TH

The Busby Babes

BY
David Sandison

This edition first published by
Parragon Book Service Ltd in 1996

Parragon Book Service Ltd
Unit 13–17 Avonbridge Trading Estate
Atlantic Road, Avonmouth
Bristol BS11 9QD

Produced by Magpie Books,
an imprint of Robinson Publishing

ISBN 0 75251 772 4

A copy of the British Library Cataloguing in Publication
Data is available from the British Library.

Typeset by Whitelaw & Palmer Ltd, Glasgow
Printed in Singapore

DEATH IN MUNICH

At three minutes past three on the afternoon of Thursday, 6 February 1958, Commander James Thain, chief pilot of a British European Airways Elizabethan 609 turbo-prop airliner, watched the instruments on his flight-deck confirm that the build-up of engine power necessary for take-off had been achieved.

Ahead of him stretched the ice-cold, slush-strewn runway of Munich's Riem Airport, a concrete strip down which he and his co-pilot, Captain Ken Rayment, had already powered the Elizabethan twice that day in failed attempts to begin the flight to Manchester, home destination of his passengers. On both occasions, they had experienced a mysterious and sudden drop in engine thrust which had forced Thain to abort take-off – the last attempt being half an hour earlier, after which the passengers had briefly returned to the airport lounge while technicians scoured the aircraft for a solution.

Nothing specific had been found, however, and now the engines seemed to be running smoothly. Convinced that the problem was nothing serious, Thain confirmed his intention to proceed and got the all-clear from the control tower. As the engine pitch rose, the pilot pushed the throttle control full forward. The Elizabethan picked up speed, dutifully accelerating in response.

Wreckage of the aircraft

Less than a minute later, the Elizabethan lay in a field, its fuselage torn apart into two separate segments, one of them embedded in the ruins of a small cottage from which its owner had miraculously managed to escape with her two tiny children.

Moments earlier, as the Elizabethan roared along the runway, some of those in the passenger section heard a noise they later described as 'like a car changing down a gear' from one of the engines. In the cockpit, Thain and Rayment watched in horror as the needle on the speed indicator suddenly and inexplicably dropped from a satisfactory 117 knots to a mere 105 – not enough to effect take-off.

Thain pushed on the throttle, but found it already at maximum. The end of the runway loomed, along with the airport's perimeter fence. The aircraft, call-signed G-ALZU-609, was doomed, as were many of those strapped into their seats, unaware of the disaster about to befall them. Only 21 of the 44 on board would survive.

And it was a disaster, not merely for the families and friends of the 23 either killed or fatally injured in the crash, but also for the untold thousands of sports fans for whom many of the casualties were idols, young Titans who had captured their imagination and loyalty by transforming the game of football into a joyful celebration of excitement and skill.

They were the remarkable Busby Babes, the young Manchester United team painstakingly created by the visionary Matt Busby out of the ruins of World War II. With an average age of only 22, they had just qualified for the semi-finals of the European Cup – the first

English team to take up the challenge of Europe's premier soccer tournament.

That milestone had been achieved by an enthralling 3-3 draw with the mighty Red Star Belgrade less than 24 hours earlier. Tired but elated, the Busby Babes, their coaching staff and a nine-man posse of top British sports writers, had been heading home from the Yugoslavian capital when their flight touched down at Munich for a routine refuelling.

Eight of those players were either killed out-right in the crash, or would die later of their injuries. They included team captain Roger Byrne, centre forward tyro Tommy Taylor and England international *wunderkind*, Duncan Edwards. Others, including Northern Ireland star Jackie Blanchflower, would never play again, so badly were they injured. A few – notably goalkeeper Harry Gregg, star forward

Dennis Viollet and teenage newcomer Bobby Charlton – would recover to help Matt Busby and his assistants begin the painful task of rebuilding a new great team from the ashes.

Busby himself would fight back from his own dreadful injuries, though it would be a long, touch-and-go recovery. And eight of those writers – including former Manchester City and England international goalie Frank Swift, writing for the *News of the World* – would never again file another breathless account of a sports event.

The Munich Crash ended a wonderful dream, and the national and international football world suffered a dreadful loss. In a few terrible minutes of chaos and carnage, the Busby Babes were no more.

MATT BUSBY:
THE MASTER-BUILDER

Matt Busby was born in the tiny mining village of Orbiston, Lanarkshire, in 1909, and grew up in a two-roomed cottage. No stranger to hardship or loss, he was devastated by the death of his father and all his uncles in the trenches of World War I, and then watched as – one by one – other members of his immediate family began emigrating to the United States in search of a better life.

By the age of 17, the young Matt was set to

follow them and was waiting for his visa quota number to come up when an attractive alternative suddenly came his way: the offer of a professional contract with Manchester City. One of the English team's Scottish scouts had spotted Busby during an appearance with Denny Hibs, a local team he had joined a few months earlier.

Early days at City weren't easy. Badly homesick, Busby was never an automatic first team choice until an injury to City's regular wing half gave him his chance to shine. He blossomed and became one of City's most dependable players – a reliability rewarded with a Scottish international cap in 1933 and membership of the City team which won the English FA Cup a year later. He would also become team captain, his leadership qualities already evident.

In 1936 Busby moved to Liverpool FC, but in 1939 – along with many fellow soccer professionals – he volunteered for military service when World War II broke out. Originally a member of the 9th Battalion of the King's Liverpool Regiment, his sporting skills were recognised by transferral to the Army Physical Training Corps and eventual promotion to the rank of sergeant-major. It was in the APTC that he cut his coaching teeth and become a regular member of a star-studded army team which would, near the war's end, tour Italy to play exhibition matches against sides from various British army detachments.

Returning to civilian life in 1945, Busby was about to rejoin Liverpool as a player and assistant to manager George Kay, when he was offered the post of manager of Manchester United. The idea was appealing – Busby was realistic about his future as a player, and the chance to call all the shots as manager proved irresistible. Also, he had come to love Manchester, so the thought of returning there had a special attraction.

An understanding Liverpool released Matt Busby from his contract and with an unprecedented five-year contract, he began the job of rebuilding Manchester United: It was a formidable task. The club's Old Trafford ground was still a tangled heap of wreckage, thanks to direct hits by German bombs in 1941, and United were forced to accept the hospitality of deadly rivals Manchester City, hiring their Maine Road stadium for home games until May 1949 when, with help from the War Damage Commission, a resurrected Old Trafford finally reopened its gates.

More serious, perhaps, was the fact that United were a hefty £15,000 in debt, which

Matt Busby

meant little or no money for Busby to buy players to replace those who, although still on the club's books, were away on military service. The squad he inherited was a solid one, however, and certainly a firm enough foundation on which to start building a team capable of matching his vision. He also proved he meant business by putting on a tracksuit to join his players in training – a revolutionary move in an era when managers tended to be imperious, remote, desk- and touchline-bound theoriticians.

As well as leading by example and so creating a very real bond with his team, Busby also brought in Jimmy Murphy, a former West Bromwich and Wales player he had met during the war. Nominally assistant manager, Murphy quickly became known as the man who wielded the stick while Busby shrewdly became the approachable and amiable face of the team. The partnership would survive until both retired in 1971- one of the most formidable double-acts in world soccer history.

When Busby took the Manchester United job in October 1945, the club was languishing at sixteenth in the First Division of the Northern League. By the end of the season they had climbed to a creditable fourth place. In February 1946 he had persuaded his chairman, James Gibson, to find £5,000 to buy Jimmy 'Brittle Bones' Delaney from Glasgow Celtic – a move many considered ill-judged, given Delaney's history of injuries and relatively advanced age. Busby was proved right, as the speedy right winger slotted effortlessly into a team which promptly began winning.

In the next season, 1946–47, with the re-sumption of a national league, United were only beaten to the championship title by the one-point advantage of Liverpool. They were also runners-up in the following two seasons, and managed to get some silverware back in the Old Trafford trophy room by winning the FA Cup in 1948, beating Blackpool in a 4-2 classic.

On the road to Wembley, United scored no less than 18 goals in their five qualifying games to confirm the quality of Busby's strike force – Delaney on the right wing, Charlie Mitten on the left, and centre forward Jack Rowley flanked by inside right Johnny Morris and inside left Stan Pearson.

Captain of the team, and a rock at right back, was Johnny Carey. Destined to be voted Footballer of the Year in 1949, Carey also uniquely played for Northern Ireland, captained the Republic of Ireland and was selected to lead a Rest of the World team which played a Great Britain side in 1947. He remained United's skipper until they finally won the League Championship in the 1951–52 season. He retired from playing in 1953, went into management and then returned to Old Trafford as a part-time scout.

Securing the League Championship, which United had not done for 41 years, guaranteed Matt Busby security of tenure in his job, made him a hero to half of Manchester and confirmed his national reputation as a brilliant manager. Since taking up the Old Trafford post, his team had been runners-up three times in succession, managed a creditable fourth place, and then returned to the second spot once more before emerging champions. And there had also been the sweet FA Cup victory in 1948.

As contented as he must have been at the end

of that season, Matt Busby believed that his career had only just begun. The rest of the footballing world hadn't seen anything yet!

BIRTH OF THE BABES

Matt Busby was keenly aware of the importance of scouts, owing his own career to a Manchester City 'stringer' who spotted his potential in the late 1920s. He quickly enlarged United's network of trusted scouts to help him find youngsters who could be moulded into the kind of players Busby and Murphy could use to take the club to greater victories.

The key men in Busby's network would be Joe Armstrong (assigned the duty of finding schoolboy talent in the north of England),

Bob Harper and Bob Bishop (keeping eagle eyes on potential stars in Belfast) and Billy Behan (taking care of business in Dublin).

Once taken on, youngsters were coaxed and groomed by coach Bert Whalley and trainer Tom Curry. They were winners of the FA Youth Cup tournament, first introduced in the 1952–53 season, for five successive years, giving Busby a formidable and reliable source of new and exciting talent. The Busby Babes had arrived, though no one had yet coined the nickname.

Matt Busby was the epitome of the 'canny' Scot when it came to the transfer market, as his purchase of the supposedly over-the-hill Delaney had proved. That shrewdness became invaluable when, in the wake of the League Championship season, he decided that the veterans in his squad had to be replaced. Good and

loyal as they were, many were ready to hang up
their boots or move on into coaching jobs or as
players with other teams. In 1950, for instance,
Jimmy Delaney had decided to return to
Scotland and play for Aberdeen. Shortly
before, fellow winger Charlie Mitten ill advis-
edly joined a rebel group of British players who
accepted lucrative offers to play in Colombia,
even though the league there had been out-
lawed by FIFA, football's international gov-
erning body.

The new wingers Busby signed were Bolton's
Harry McShane and Johnny Berry, a
Birmingham City player who had impressed
Busby a year earlier when he'd hustled,
bustled – and scored a delightful goal – at Old
Trafford. Bought for £25,000, Berry scored
six goals in his first season and went on to
make almost 300 League and Cup appearances for United, and to score another 43

goals, until the severe head injuries he suffered at Munich ended his career.

By the end of that Championship season, United also had a new outside left – the 20-year-old Roger Byrne. The first graduate of Busby's youth training academy, and so the first true Busby Babe, Byrne began his first team career at left back, but was switched to left wing for the last six games of the season.

Byrne scored 7 goals in those matches, staking a claim to key roles both in Matt Busby's future plans and those of the English national squad selectors. On the club front, he returned to his original left back position, using his natural speed and strength to start and take part in attacking moves every bit as ably as he served in defence – a rare range of skills in those days.

Roger Byrne

He played almost 300 League and Cup games for United before being killed at Munich. He won no less than 33 successive international caps after first being picked for the England team in 1954. Aged only 28 when he died, Byrne had not been told that he was due to become a father for the first time. His wife Joy would give birth to a son, Roger, eight months after the crash.

When United lost six of their first 11 games in the 1952–53 season, Busby knew he had to act fast, acquire new players on the open market and bring on some of the youngsters that his scouts had brought to the club in preceding years.

The transfer market (and the sum of £29,999, fixed by Busby to avoid giving the player a £30,000 price tag) yielded the talents of Tommy Taylor, a strong and combative centre forward bought from Barnsley to replace Jack Rowley. Like Byrne, Taylor matched his United form with an England international career which produced 19 caps. In the course of representing his country, Taylor scored 16 goals, including two hat-tricks.

At club level, Taylor played 163 League games for United, scoring 112 goals in the process. In 1956, when they regained the League Championship, Tommy Taylor scored 25 times in his 33 appearances, while his tally of 'assists' was formidable as he selflessly helped colleagues to bury the ball in the back of the net.

Roger Byrne's new partner at right back was Bill Foulkes, who had followed his father down the pit as a youngster in St Helens, but had been spotted and picked up by United while playing as an amateur for Whiston Boys

Club. He became a full-time professional and won his regular first team place in 1953.

Foulkes proved to be one of Manchester United's most durable players, clocking up some 600 appearances for the club during a First Division career which lasted a remarkable 18 years and resulted in a collection of four League Championship medals, one FA Cup winner's medal and – in 1968, when United finally won the tournament – a European Cup medal. As one of the Munich survivors who linked the Busby Babes and later teams, Bill Foulkes also became team captain for a while.

When he finally retired in 1970, Foulkes was appointed youth coach at Old Trafford before both managing and playing in the United States and Norway. A measure of the high regard in which he was held by his fellow veterans, was his election as the first chairman of the association of ex-Manchester United players when it was founded.

But the 1952–53 season would go down in history as the one in which the most famous Busby Babe of all – left half Duncan Edwards – made his transition from the youth squad to the first team. His debut, against Cardiff City at Old Trafford on Easter Monday, 1953, was achieved at the incredibly young age of 15 years, 285 days.

Taken into the United fold when he was just 14, Edwards formed a formidable mid-field partnership with Eddie 'Snake Hips' Colman at right half and centre half Mark Jones. Born in Dudley, Worcestershire, Edwards was a large-framed and intimidating figure who had played in a number of positions as a schoolboy international – centre forward, wing half, centre half and inside forward – with accomplished ease.

Described by Jimmy Murphy as 'the greatest of them all', Duncan Edwards quickly became the mid-field rock on which United's first lines of defence and attack depended, a young man able to match controlled aggression in his tackles with an astute footballing brain capable of creating gaps for others, and delivering the ball to them once those gaps appeared. Few players at any level were able to rob Edwards of the ball once it was at his feet.

During the next five years Edwards emerged as one of England's most exciting, gifted and dynamic international players, making the first of an eventual 19 appearances in the national team's 7–2 defeat of Scotland at Wembley when he was just 17 – the country's youngest-ever full cap. It was widely assumed that he would eventually succeed Billy Wright as England captain.

There is no doubt in the minds of those who thrilled to the spectacle of Duncan Edwards in full flow – whether they be United fans, opposing clubs' supporters or international commentators and players – that his death from the injuries he suffered in Munich, robbed the world of a very special player whose already distinguished career was still in its infancy. He was only 21 when he died, but had already played a key role in United's League Championships in 1956 and 1957 and their achievement in reaching the FA Cup Final in 1957.

Manchester United's regular goal-keeping duties had already been given to another youngster by the beginning of the 1952–53 season as Ray Wood replaced Reg Allen.

Signed as a teenager from Darlington in 1949, he had deputised for Allen and his predecessor, Jack Crompton, before Busby decided to promote him.

Wood proved to be as brave as he was able, in the 1957 Cup Final when his cheekbone was smashed in a collision with Aston Villa's Peter McParland. Wood was carried off on a stretcher and, as substitutes were not allowed at this time, United were reduced to ten men. Mid-fielder Jackie Blanchflower became the goalkeeper and although the team physio, Ted Dalton, decreed that the still-dazed Wood was unfit to play, he readily returned to play in an approximate outside right position, merely to keep United at full numerical strength. His contribution, needless to say, was limited mainly to retaining possession of the ball when it came his way until someone fit could do something useful with it!

Wood eventually resumed his proper position when Villa were 2–1 ahead and Matt Busby needed Blanchflower back at centre half to make the chance of an equaliser feasible. Unfortunately, the gamble, and Wood's bravery, proved to be in vain. United were unable to improve the scoreline and so missed out on the rare chance of the League and FA Cup double, a feat everyone was sure they would accomplish easily.

Ray Wood went on to play in all but one of United's 1955–56 Championship games and collected a second League Championship medal in 1957. Edged out of the first team by Harry Gregg shortly before Munich, Wood was in the ill-fated party which went to Belgrade. Fortunate to suffer relatively minor injuries in the crash, he played on, though his long-term future lay with Huddersfield Town, Bradford City and Barnsley before he began a coaching career which took him to Cyprus, the Middle East and Africa. He also won three English international caps.

THE BABES GROW UP

The transitional 1952–53 season was never likely to bring any trophies to Old Trafford, though the mix of wise old birds and fledglings managed a creditable eighth place in the League Championship, won by Arsenal. The following year, which saw the regular first team blooding of Ulsterman Jackie Blanchflower, local boy Dennis Viollet and 20-year-old Jeff Whitefoot, United achieved fourth spot in the Championship, won by Wolverhampton Wanderers.

Viollet

Jackie Blanchflower, the under-rated younger brother of Danny, the Tottenham Hotspur captain who won a record 56 international caps for Northern Ireland in a distinguished career, made only one first team appearance in 1952–53, but became a vital cog in the Busby machine in 1953–54, during which he played 27 games and scored 13 times. The following year, when United finished the season in fifth place (with Chelsea taking the title), Blanchflower took the field 29 times, increasing his goal tally on a further ten occasions.

In 1955–56, when United regained the League Championship, Jackie played 18 times and scored only 3 goals. However, his relative lack of scoring success hardly mattered in a goal feast of a season which saw Tommy Taylor knock 25 in and Dennis Viollet put a further 20 past various hapless 'keepers. United were on an unprecedented roll that year, scoring 83 goals.

When they retained the league title in 1956–57, the Busby Babes went an unparalleled step further with a season goal tally of 103. Troubled by injuries that year, Jackie made only 11 appearances and scored no goals, but Viollet slotted in 16, Taylor added another 22, while two newcomers – teenagers Bobby Charlton and Billy Whelan – scored 10 and 26 respectively.

With Tommy Taylor all-conquering at centre forward, the arrival of Dennis Viollet in 1953 gave Matt Busby a front-line double act which proved unrivalled in the English league. Destined to inherit Taylor's position after Munich, Viollet was actually born near Maine Road and had been a loyal Manchester City supporter from childhood. However,

Charlton

the combined cajolery of scout Joe Armstrong
and Jimmy Murphy – plus the avuncular
persuasion of ex-City player Matt Busby –
had persuaded the talented youngster to sign
for 'the enemy'.

Although Viollet's scoring record between
1953 and the Munich disaster helped the
Busby Babes to achieve a remarkable turn-
around during those six heady years, Dennis
Viollet played an even greater and more
important role in helping rebuild Manchester
United after the tragedy. He recovered
quickly from his injuries, and scored 21 goals
in the 1958–59 season before breaking Jack
Rowley's club record of 30 league goals (set
in 1952), by slotting 32 into the net in 1960.

Remarkably, Viollet won only two England
international caps despite his outstanding
League and FA Cup career, (159 goals in 259

appearances over a ten-year period). He left Old Trafford in 1962 to play for Stoke, where he helped them gain promotion from the Second Division, before winning an Irish FA Cup-winner's medal with Linfield. He then emigrated to the United States, where he played and coached.

The dynamic duo of Taylor and Viollet were not the only players capable of compiling formidable goal-scoring totals. The introduction of Billy Whelan to the first team in 1954, another brilliant youngster who'd been signed as a teenager, gave the Busby Babes yet another supreme match-winner.

Better known in his native Dublin as Liam, Billy Whelan was a graduate of the city's Home Farm club, a footballing academy which proved a fruitful source of recruits for Manchester United through the years. Notionally an inside forward, there to supply Taylor and Viollet with the ammunition to blast in goals, Whelan would prove – like so many of the Busby Babes – a player capable of much more.

He quickly became an able supply source for his team-mates, and was also no slouch when it came to taking advantage of any goal-scoring opportunities which came his way. In the four seasons he played at Old Trafford before losing his life in Munich, Billy Whelan made 96 League and Cup appearances and scored 52 goals in the process. His pace, vision, control and selflessness were also called on four times for the Republic of Ireland national team.

The balance which made the Manchester United attack so formidable was created, finally, by the presence of Johnny Berry – still at outside left – and David Pegg, the team's

regular left winger since 1953, recruited from
Doncaster. During his five years with United,
Pegg made 127 appearances in the first team,
putting his name on the score-sheet 24 times.
Selected only once for England international
honours (against the Republic of Ireland), it is
a measure of Manchester United's dominance
that his England team-mates on that day
included Roger Byrne, Duncan Edwards and
Tommy Taylor.

Last – and certainly not least – was the
increasingly important figure of yet another
graduate of the United youth squad. He was
Bobby Charlton, a Northumbrian lad scouted
and signed by Manchester in 1953, when he
was just 16-years-old.

A member of the notable Milburn footballing
family, (uncles Jim and George had enjoyed
illustrious careers with Leeds, as would his

older brother, Jack, while his cousin was none other than Jackie Milburn, hero and superstar centre forward for Newcastle United for most of the 1950s), Bobby made his League debut in 1956 when he scored 2 of United's goals as they beat Charlton Athletic 4–2.

Despite scoring 10 times in his 14 appearances in the 1956–57 season, it was not until a few months before the Munich crash that Charlton became Matt Busby's regular first team choice. Until then, his name tended to be included on the team-sheet only when Dennis Viollet and Tommy Taylor were indisposed. Ample proof of the riches Busby now had at his disposal, lies in the fact that a young and undeniably brilliant player like Bobby Charlton could be eased into the team so gradually.

During the fateful 1957–58 season, Bobby

Arsenal v Manchester United, 1 February 1958

Charlton played on 21 occasions and scored a
further 8 goals, 2 of them in the 3–3 draw
with Red Star Belgrade which put Manchester United into the semi-finals of the
European Cup.

Bobby Charlton survived the Munich crash,
and went on to become one of Manchester
United and England's most distinguished
servants. When he finally retired from playing
in 1973, he had scored 198 goals in 606
League appearances, helped his club win the
Championship in 1957, 1965 and 1967, the
FA Cup in 1963, the European Cup in 1968,
been voted English and European Footballer
of the Year in 1966 – the year he and brother
Jack played in England's victorious World
Cup team – and scored 49 goals in the course
of earning 106 international caps.

However, all this lay in the future, as did his

Matt Busby and Bobby Charlton

awards of the OBE in 1969 and the CBE in 1974. As a Busby Babe, Bobby Charlton was content to be part of the most thrilling footballing team Britain had ever seen.

It was time to take that team into Europe and pitch it against the cream of the continent.

THE BABES IN EUROPE

The Busby Babes' first excursion into Europe came in the 1956–57 season, when their League Championship win of the season before qualified them for participation in the relatively new but prestigious European Cup. Designed to pitch the leading club teams of Europe's various national leagues against each other, the tournament had been introduced in the 1955–56 season when the mighty Real Madrid emerged as champions – a title they would retain a record four times in succession.

As English League champions for 1954–55, Chelsea had been invited to take part in the inaugural European Cup. Submitting to the will of the blazer-clad dinosaurs in the Football Association and the Football League, who considered the added burden of European fixtures would detract from the domestic game, Chelsea had declined to enter.

When Manchester United received their invitation, Matt Busby discovered that the League's attitude remained firmly set against the tournament. However, this time the great and good men of the FA had decided it was perhaps a good idea after all for an English club to wave the flag abroad, even though such a decision had nothing to do with them, given that the tournament was solely for League champions!

The FA's approval was good enough for Busby, who desperately wanted his players to be able to play against – and learn from – the superb continental sides who had qualified. He accepted the invitation eagerly and Manchester United began to prepare for their first meeting with Europe's finest.

The team's arrival on the international scene would prove as triumphant as it was dramatic. Drawn against the Belgian champions Anderlecht in the first round, United travelled to Brussels in September 1956, where goals from Dennis Viollet and Tommy Taylor (who else?) made them 2–1 victors in the first leg. It was a confident start from a side who came to be nicknamed 'The Red Devils' by admiring Europeans.

That admiration quickly turned to awe when the two teams met again at Maine Road two weeks later (Old Trafford's floodlighting system was still not fully operational), and the Belgians were smashed out of the tournament by a fantastic goal blitz. During 90 minutes which a dazed Matt Busby described as 'the greatest thrill in a lifetime of soccer', Viollet scored 4 goals, Taylor added 3 of his own, Billy Whelan put 2 in, and Johnny Berry slotted another into the net to make the final scoreline 10–1. Alarm bells began to ring all over Europe.

The next round found United up against the West German champions Borussia Dort-mund. At home, on 17 October, Viollet scored 2 and David Pegg 1 to give United a 3–2 win – enough to put them into the last eight when the November away game ended in a goal-less draw.

The quarter-finals saw United pitched against

Spain's Athletico Bilbao. No one believed these games were going to be anything less than a mighty tussle, and so it proved. Drawn away in the first leg in January 1957, United found themselves at the wrong end of a 3–5 scoreline on a mud-clogged pitch which – aided by flurries of snow during the game – must have helped them feel very much at home! Trailing 3–0 at half-time, a stern lecture from Matt Busby and Jimmy Murphy in the dressing room was enough to energise a Manchester team staring ignominious defeat in the face.

Second half goals from Whelan, Viollet and Taylor helped spare United's blushes, but 2 more from Bilbao left the Busby Babes with a mountainous task in the home leg, to be played on 6 February. Few – except Busby, Murphy and the players themselves – gave United any chance of making up the 2 goal deficit, especially as Bilbao were expected to play 11 men in defence.

This is pretty much what happened at Maine Road. United, however, were not going to let a small thing like a brick wall stand in their way. The helpless Bilbaons suffered wave after wave of attacks as United fought to score the 3 unanswered goals they needed to stay in Europe. They remained empty-handed until just before half-time, when Duncan Edwards blasted a long range shot which a Bilbao defender could only block with his foot and steer into the path of Dennis Viollet. He didn't miss.

Celebrations at 2 more goals early in the second half turned to groans when Whelan and Viollet were adjudged to be offside. Albert Deutsch, the West German referee, was not a popular man and his parentage was balefully called into question by furious United fans. The Maine Road groundsmen also came under suspicion when a Tommy Taylor shot was stopped by a goal post in the 70th minute. Two minutes later, the goal was found to be of regulation width after all, when another Taylor blast buried itself safely in the net.

The tension was unreal as the seconds ticked away. With only two minutes left on the clock, Tommy Taylor once more made a break through the Bilbao ranks, reached the corner flag and looked up to see Johnny Berry waiting in the goal mouth. One sweet pass direct to Berry's feet and the vital third goal was scored. As Maine Road erupted in cele- bration, it was Jimmy Murphy's turn to describe the preceding 90 minutes as 'my greatest game in football'.

It was exactly 12 months, to the day, before Commander James Thain would try to take off from Munich Airport.

Ironically, the BEA Elizabethan which flew the Busby Babes to Spain for their first semi-final meeting with European Cup-holders Real Madrid on 11 April 1957, was piloted by Captain Ken Rayment, the co-pilot who would lose his life at Munich.

If the prospect of facing the awesome might of a Real Madrid team, which featured the likes of superstar centre forward and captain Alfredo di Stefano, and deadly strikers like Gento, Mateos and Kopa, was not enough to intimidate the Manchester United squad, Real's vast Bernabeu Stadium was every bit as awe-inspiring: tier upon tier of seats, every one of them occupied, with 120,000 hysterical fans who made the roar of an Old

Trafford crowd sound like the murmur of a gentleman's club lounge.

Strangely, Matt Busby elected to give Eddie Colman the impossible task of marking di Stefano, not Duncan Edwards as widely predicted. He wanted Edwards free to help launch counter-attacks, and although Colman stuck to the Real skipper like a shadow, United found themselves out-run, out-passed and frankly out-classed from the off. They also found themselves 2 goals behind before Tommy Taylor pulled one back.

A single-goal deficit for the return match would have been a manageable hurdle to overcome, but Real hadn't finished giving United a severe lesson. A three-pronged attack featuring Gento, Riall and Mateos ended with Billy Foulkes unable to do more than parry a shot in the direction of Mateos.

He seized his chance and drove the ball past a despairing Ray Wood.

It was a subdued bunch of Babes who returned to England and the reality of League football. Back home, however, there was room for some confident optimism. United had already booked themselves into the FA Cup Final at Wembley on 4 May by beating Birmingham City 2-0 at Hillsborough. Victory over Luton by the same score two days after the Real game, meant that they had also retained their League Championship with an unbeatable lead over their closest rivals, Tottenham, even with five League games still to play. Remember, this was the year United put 103 goals past their opponents.

It was also comforting for Matt Busby to know that his decision to play in Europe had been vindicated, completely demolishing all

the League's arguments that European participation would put too much strain on a team
with a hectic domestic schedule. Manchester
United stood on the verge, not only of the
elusive League and FA Cup double, but also –
if they could beat Real Madrid at Maine
Road on 25 April – in the running for a
unique and glorious treble.

It was a big 'if' though, and proved too much,
even for the mighty Busby Babes. Although
United forced a creditable 2–2 draw with
Real, with Dennis Viollet and Bobby
Charlton the heroes on the night, it wasn't
enough. United were out of the European
Cup with a 3–5 aggregate score. Although
they had done incredibly well in their first
European adventure, the treble was no longer
attainable.

The domestic double also proved elusive.

When Aston Villa's Peter McParland crashed into Ray Wood at Wembley on 4 May, that triumph was also suddenly out of reach.

As Busby and his Babes began a well-deserved few weeks' summer break before getting down to the business of the 1957–58 season, with an away game against Leicester City on 24 August, they at least had the satisfaction of knowing that their League title guaranteed that they would be playing in Europe once more.

THE MUNICH YEAR

The Busby Babes began the 1957–58 season
with a purple streak which produced six wins
(scoring 27 goals and conceding only four),
one draw (3–3 with Everton), and only two
defeats (0–4 to Bolton and 1–2 to Blackpool).
The last domestic game before their first
European Cup match saw them play hosts to
Arsenal and warm up by slotting 4 past the
North London team, who could only answer
with 2.

Matt Busby also had the luxury, at this stage,

of playing the same 11 men every time: Wood, Foulkes, Byrne, Blanchflower, Edwards, Berry, Whelan, Taylor, Viollet and Pegg. The Babes were up and running.

Their first European encounter, on 25 September, saw an on-form and on-song United travel to the Republic of Ireland to begin a demolition of local League champions, Shamrock Rovers. Freddie Goodwin stood in for Eddie Colman in a side which ran away with a 6–0 victory, thanks to two goals apiece from Dennis Viollet and Irishman Billy Whelan, and one each from Berry and Pegg.

Shamrock made a better job of it on 2 October when they put the ball past Wood twice, but 2 more goals from Viollet, and 1 from David Pegg, ensured that United went comfortably through to a second round meeting with the much stronger Czech champions, Dukla Prague, on 21 November. United had the advantage of playing their first leg at home, in front of a crowd whose rousing support rival managers reckoned was powerful enough to guarantee at least one goal from Busby's teams.

Busby decided to rest some key players for the next League game after the first Irish meeting, at eventual champions Wolverhampton Wanderers on 28 September. He played the durable mid-fielder/defender Wilf McGuinness, yet another fast-rising product of United's youth programme, instead of Roger Byrne, and also gave John Doherty, Goodwin and Bobby Charlton a chance to shine. Although Doherty managed to score, Wolves emerged as 3–1 victors.

The next seven League games, (against Aston Villa, Nottingham Forest, Portsmouth, West

Bromwich Albion, Burnley, Preston North End and Sheffield Wednesday), saw United rack up four wins, one draw and two losses. Not bad, but a worrying aspect of the losses was the fact that Portsmouth had put 3 past Wood, while West Brom had managed 4 in a seven-goal thriller which United believed they had sewn up. No one, not least Matt Busby, blamed Wood solely for these goals, but the suspicion lurked that he had not completely recovered from his Cup Final injuries.

While Matt Busby began a hush-hush shopping expedition, which would end with the signing of Doncaster Rover's Northern Ireland international Harry Gregg, Ray Wood continued to guard the goal (except on one occasion, when his understudy, David Gaskell, replaced him) until 21 December, when Gregg took over for good.

Wood was not over-busy for the first home leg game against Dukla Prague on 21 November which United won 3–0, thanks to goals from Taylor, Pegg and Colin Webster, standing in for Viollet, as he had done for Billy Whelan in the second Shamrock Rovers tie. Although the Babes lost the return game in Prague 0–1 on 4 December, they once again had the heartening prospect of playing at home for the first of their two quarter-final matches against the Yugoslavian champions, Red Star Belgrade.

The domestic season continued to deliver mixed fortunes, however, and while United managed to win three of their next nine games (against Newcastle, Leicester and Luton), they could only draw with Birmingham City, Luton and Manchester City. More worryingly, they also lost to Tottenham and Chelsea. Points were

Busby briefs the team in Belgrade

dropped everywhere while Wolverhampton Wanderers started to pull away.

On 14 January 1958, with Harry Gregg now in goal and a forward ensemble which boasted Morgans, Charlton, Taylor, Viollet and Albert Scanlon, United emerged 2–1 victors in a tight game against Red Star which proved that the second leg, to be played in Belgrade on 5 February, was going to be a tough one. United's goals had come from Bobby Charlton and Eddie Colman.

Busby's young stars departed for Belgrade, leaving the English game with a memorable example of their heady blend of skill and defiant determination. On 1 February they travelled to London to face the challenge of an on-form Arsenal. It was to prove a match which everyone lucky enough to see would

cite in defence of the much-maligned English
game for many years to come.

Although shaken by news of the sudden death
of United director George Whittaker only
hours before kick-off, United had forged 3–0
ahead before allowing Arsenal back into the
game. The score stood tantalisingly at 4–4
until the Babes performed a one-bound
escape to emerge as 5–4 winners.

Roger Byrne was nursing a niggling injury
when United arrived in Belgrade, but a prac-
tice session on a water-logged training pitch
confirmed he was fit enough to play. He took
the field as skipper of the already legendary
team that Red Star's fans were desperate to
see in action. No one knew that it would be
for the last time.

United took the lead in just two minutes,

Tommy Taylor racing away towards the Red Star goal from his own half. Drawing the defence, he passed to an unmarked Viollet who took his chance in almost arrogant fashion. Within 20 minutes, despite Ken Morgans being a walking wounded participant, thanks to a Red Star player's studs proving tougher than his right thigh, United were 2–0 up, courtesy of a Bobby Charlton thunderbolt.

Amazingly, the stadium remained a riot of sound as large numbers of Red Star supporters began cheering every tricky move, every display of skill that the Babes used to bewilder the home team. They were in the presence of something special and were prepared to acknowledge the fact with deserved applause. Just before half-time, Charlton beat Red Star's 'keeper Beara with another 25-yard screamer. And it was only the linesman's flag

signalling off-side which robbed the youngster of a memorable hat-trick seconds before
the referee whistled for the break.

Whatever Red Star's coach said to his men in
the dressing room, it obviously worked. They
came out firing on all cylinders, making the
score 3–1 two minutes later when Secularac
floated a deceptive ball over Harry Gregg,
who had come off his line. Red Star launched
attack after attack, with United's defence
stretched time and again.

The outstretched leg of Bill Foulkes caught
Red Star's Zebec in the goal area, and let him
translate the resulting penalty kick into the
home team's second goal. With United now
having to deal with occasional flurries of
snowballs as Yugoslavian supporters got
behind their team, Red Star won a free kick
just outside the box, when Harry Gregg slith-

The team lines up before the Red Star match

ered outside the goal area with the ball after making a save. Kostic threaded the ball through United's wall into the top corner of the net.

The Manchester United dressing room was a strange mixture of disappointment and elation as the team nursed their aches, pains and wounds. The disappointment was at having let a 3–0 lead slip to a 3–3 draw. The elation came from knowing that it was still enough to put them through, once again, to the European Cup semi-finals and a meeting with the Italian superstars of AC Milan.

There was also satisfaction in the sincere praise and congratulations they received from Red Star players, coaching staff and Yugoslavian sports writers who wished them nothing but good fortune for the future. United had made a lot of friends and fans that day. There was an official dinner that evening for both teams, but Matt Busby and his brilliant Babes were already looking forward to flying home the next day to a match, only two days later, against Wolverhampton Wanderers, now a worrying four points ahead of them in the League.

Roger Byrne, Tommy Taylor, Duncan Edwards, David Pegg, Mark Jones, Eddie Colman, Billy Whelan and Geoff Bent would not travel any further than the refuelling stop at Munich.

THE CRASH – AND AFTER

Every disaster has its heroes and its miracles, and the crash which would soon simply be known by the shorthand 'Munich', was no exception.

In the minutes which followed the disaster, goalkeeper Harry Gregg, team-mate Bill Foulkes, *Daily Mail* photographer Peter Howard and Ted Ellyard, his telegraphist, were principal among the survivors who struggled back into the wreckage to rescue others, despite the overwhelming threat of

Captain Thain (left) and surviving crew members

fire from the Elizabethan's ruptured fuel tanks.

Prompt action by pilot James Thain – who would subsequently be cleared of any blame for a crash caused by a build-up of ice on the plane's wings – and radio officer George Rogers helped extinguish five small fires in and around the wreckage. But it was Harry Gregg, unaware that the risk of explosion had been averted, who bravely scrambled back to save the life of the 20-month-old daughter of Mrs Vera Lukic, wife of the Yugoslavian air attaché in London, who had been allowed to hitch a ride on the charter flight. On his second visit, Gregg saved Mrs Lukic herself.

Thrown clear of the crash, a shoeless Bill Foulkes stumbled back to help his friends. It was he who found Matt Busby, still strapped in his seat. Obviously badly hurt, Busby was

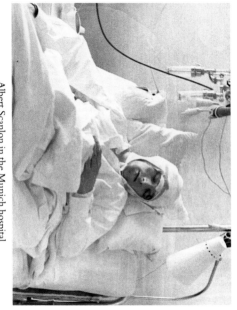

Albert Scanlon in the Munich hospital

comforted by Foulkes and Gregg, who kept his icy hands warm by rubbing them.

As rescue teams began rushing in to help, the full horror of the situation became clear. Bodies of dead and dying people lay everywhere, though no one knew for sure just how high the eventual death toll would be.

There seemed no explanation as to why some survived when those sitting next to them died, nor how some who were thrown from the crash lived. Bill Foulkes escaped almost without a scratch while Albert Scanlon – with whom he'd begun playing cards as the plane attempted its doomed take-off – suffered severe leg and head injuries. Bobby Charlton was thrown 70 yards from the crash scene, but escaped with a relatively minor head wound and shock.

Frank Taylor, the northern sports columnist of *The News Chronicle,* also survived, though his 21 fractures put him in the care of Munich's Rechts der Isar Hospital's brilliant surgical team for a long time. However, it soon became known that he and Peter Howard were the only writers who had escaped. Friends and rivals who died were Henry Rose (*Daily Express*), Alf Clarke (*Manchester Evening Chronicle*), Don Davies (*Manchester Guardian*), George Follows (*Daily Herald*), Tom Jackson (*Manchester Evening News*), Archie Ledbrooke (*Daily Mirror*), Frank Swift (*News of the World*) and Eric Thompson (*Daily Mail*).

Taylor, who eventually resumed his distinguished career and was awarded an OBE in 1979, was also able to write a harrowing eyewitness account of the crash in a best-selling book, *The Day A Team Died.*

It was not only the cream of their gifted players that Manchester United FC lost that afternoon in Munich. Club secretary Walter Crickman was also killed, as were Tom Curry, the first team trainer, and coach Bert Whalley, two of the men who had done so much to help Matt Busby build and develop his beloved Babes.

The harsh reality was that Roger Byrne, Geoff Bent, David Pegg, Mark Jones, Eddie Colman, Tommy Taylor and Billy Whelan had been killed outright, while Johnny Berry and Duncan Edwards were fighting for their lives, as was the flight's co-pilot, Ken Rayment.

Two weeks after the crash, when doctors were starting to think he might pull through, Duncan Edwards finally succumbed to his injuries. The people of his home town,

Dudley, would mark his glorious but tragically short life with a permanent memorial in the form of a stained glass window in St Francis in the Priory Church. Ken Rayment also died, his body unable to deal with the trauma of being crushed by wreckage.

Johnny Berry and Jackie Blanchflower eventually recoverd from their injuries but were unable to resume their playing careers, whilst Albert Scanlon, Dennis Viollet, Ken Morgans, Bobby Charlton and Ray Wood all played their part in reshaping Manchester United's future.

For a long while it was feared that Matt Busby would also die, his chest crushed and foot broken by the impact. Desperately ill for a long time, photographs of him in an oxygen tent only served to heighten the sense of tragedy everyone – friends and friendly foes alike –

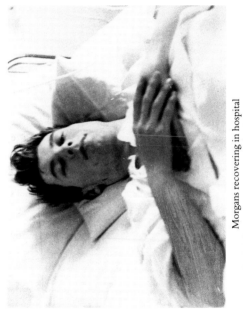

Morgans recovering in hospital

experienced as the news of the disaster spread.

So unprecedented was the Munich crash that there were no guidelines to dictate what should happen as far as the rest of the football season was concerned. Even as the mourning began, the Football League wisely decided to postpone United's scheduled meeting with Wolves, while a number of teams were quick to offer the unconditional loan of players to help them out of their awful predicament. On the following Saturday, all soccer and most rugby games in Britain began with a minute's silence in tribute to the fallen.

The matter of who would pick up the reins was easily solved by Jimmy Murphy, Matt Busby's able lieutenant, who was not with the team for the Belgrade game. As manager of the Welsh national team, he had been given leave of absence for a fixture which clashed

The new team, March 1958

Matt Busby limps from the hospital

with the Babes' European trip. He took charge until Matt Busby returned home to a hero's welcome on 18 April 1958.

At Old Trafford, the gymnasium was used to house the coffins of those who had died, so that thousands of supporters could make their last tearful farewells. The funeral of Henry Rose, then one of the country's best-loved sports journalists, brought central Manchester to a halt, so many thousands more wished to pay their respects.

There was to be no fairytale ending. Despite the massive wave of sympathy which carried Manchester United through the rest of the season and – unbelievably – to a second successive FA Cup Final, they lost that 0–2 to Bolton Wanderers. And, while goals from Dennis Viollet and Ernie Taylor gave United a notable 2–0 win over AC Milan in the

European Cup at Old Trafford on 8 May, the away leg eight days later saw them succumb to a 4–0 defeat and exit from their second European adventure.

In the League Championship, United managed to struggle to a creditable ninth place by season's end, but it was Wolverhampton Wanderers who won the right to represent English football in the following season's European tournament.

Manchester United, with Matt Busby once again fully fit and back at the helm, steered themselves to a wonderful second place in the 1958–59 League Championship, won once more by Wolverhampton Wanderers. It was not until 1965 that they would be champions again.

They repeated that success in 1966–67,

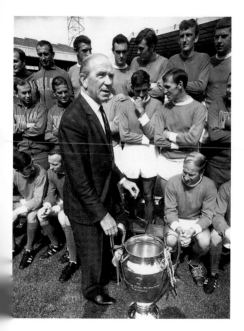

Winners of the European Cup, 1968

Safely back from the next flight together, May 1959

regained the chance to shine in Europe and, on 29 May 1968, beat Benfica 4–1 at Wembley finally to hold the European Cup in their hands. Two of the goals scored that day came off the boots of Bobby Charlton. One of the men who posed with him for victory photographs was a fellow survivor of Munich, Bill Foulkes.

Oh yes – and Matt Busby, of course. Two years later, when he retired as team manager, Matt Busby would rightly be knighted for his services to the game he loved, and to which he had brought so much.

Together with Jimmy Murphy, they all had every reason to pause and consider what might have been, and remember the friends they lost at Munich ten years earlier. A team, and a dream, may have died that day. But their legend lives on.